21st
Century
Skills Library

GLOBAL PERSPECTIVES

RACISM

Katie Marsico

Cherry Lake Publishing
Ann Arbor, Michigan

CHERRY
LAKE
Publishing

Published in the United States of America by Cherry Lake Publishing
Ann Arbor, Michigan
www.cherrylakepublishing.com

Content Adviser: David Stovall, PhD, Associate Professor of Educational Policy Studies
and African-American Studies, University of Illinois, Chicago, Illinois

Photo Credits: Cover and page 1, Courtesy of Jon Levine, People's Organization for
Progress; page 4, © POPPERFOTO/Alamy; page 7, © Mike Abrahams/Alamy; page
9, © Laurence Gough, used under license from Shutterstock, Inc.; page 10, © Ingvald
Kaldhussater, used under license from Shutterstock, Inc.; page 12, © Pictorial Press Ltd/
Alamy; page 13, © POPPERFOTO/Alamy; page 16, © Danita Delimont/Alamy; page 18,
© Elena Elisseeva, used under license from Shutterstock, Inc.; page 20, Courtesy of Jon
Levine, People's Organization for Progress; page 23, © iStockphoto.com/aldomurillo;
page 24, © iStockphoto.com/bonniej; page 26, © Keren Su/China Span/Alamy

Map by XNR Productions Inc

.

Library of Congress Cataloging-in-Publication Data
Marsico, Katie, 1980–
Racism / by Katie Marsico.
   p. cm.—(Global perspectives)
Includes index.
ISBN-13: 978-1-60279-134-3
ISBN-10: 1-60279-134-1
1. Racism—Juvenile literature. I. Title. II. Series.
HT1521.M2814 2008
305.8—dc22   2007041478

*Cherry Lake Publishing would like to acknowledge the work of
The Partnership for 21st Century Skills.
Please visit www.21stcenturyskills.org for more information.*

TABLE of CONTENTS

CHAPTER ONE

A MEETING TO END MISUNDERSTANDINGS

Army troops were called out to protect the first black students to attend Central High School in Little Rock, Arkansas, in 1957.

Kayla Thompson nervously looked over the note cards that lay on the cafeteria table in front of her. She had made a long but exciting journey from Atlanta, Georgia, to Interlaken, Switzerland. She was there to attend a student **summit** on global issues. Kayla was one of several people contributing to a working group focused on ending **racism**—a goal she was eager to see accomplished.

Because the Thompsons were African American, Kayla felt she knew only too well what it was like to be **discriminated** against, to be judged unfairly simply because of the color of her skin. She had often heard her grandmother talk about what it was like to live in the southern United States during the 1950s and 1960s. Back then, blacks routinely faced racial **prejudice** in the workforce and in schools. Things had gotten better over time, but Kayla knew that racism still existed. She was determined to play a role in combating it.

As she jotted down a couple of last-minute thoughts on her note cards, someone tapped on her shoulder. "It's time to go back in now," said a boy who had come up behind her. "You're Kayla, right?"

Kayla smiled back, though she was slightly annoyed at the intrusion. She had heard this **delegate**, whose name was Omar bin Ahmad, speaking earlier in the day. He made some excellent points, but Kayla wondered what he truly felt about her—or any other woman— attending the convention after she learned he was from Pakistan. She knew that women in **Islamic** countries had far fewer rights than men. Besides, she had heard her father say that, while he didn't personally

Learning & Innovation Skills

Is there any way to ensure that the Web isn't used to spread racism? Over the past several years, everyone from world leaders to Internet service providers (ISPs) have begun to question what can be done to stop individuals who turn to their computers to promote racial **intolerance**.

A lot of people think that the men and women responsible for posting racist content via e-mail or Web pages should receive fines or be legally punished for their actions. Others argue that this response violates a person's freedom of speech. What do you think? Should people be able to post whatever they want on Web sites?

have anything against Pakistanis, it was well-known that many were anti-American.

Omar seemed nice enough, but could he honestly put aside those kinds of sentiments for the sake of the summit? In the weeks leading up to the convention, the students had exchanged e-mails. They shared reports by **sociologists** and news clips profiling the effects of racism in their countries. It was clear that racism had existed for an incredibly long time and that more and more people were taking a stand against it as the years passed. But there still was quite a bit of work to be done in order to wipe it out completely.

What the delegates to the summit had to determine was the most effective way for people everywhere to win the war against this social problem. Kayla hated to admit it, but she wondered if a country such as Pakistan was ready to take up that challenge. Her doubts echoed through her mind as she began walking toward the meeting room with Omar.

Two women get water from a well in Pakistan.

"Do you miss your home?" she asked awkwardly, wondering if she should have struck up a lighthearted discussion about the weather instead.

"Very much! I know we're making a huge difference here, and it's a wonderful opportunity to come to Interlaken, but my sister is graduating from medical school this week. She's going to move to Chicago in a few months to work at a hospital there."

Kayla blinked. Medical school? But didn't most Pakistani men disapprove of women working outside the home? And why would a Pakistani woman want to leave her country to live with a bunch of Americans? "What does your father say about all this?" she blurted out, before she thought better of it.

"We're all incredibly proud of her, of course. Besides, I've never been there, but I hear Chicago is an amazing city." He must have seen Kayla's disbelieving stare because he laughed good-naturedly as they took their seats. "Oh, I see! You must think that everyone in Pakistan—in *every* Muslim country for that matter—doesn't believe women should have the same opportunities as men. And that we all despise America, of course!"

Kayla blushed and pulled out her note cards. "I didn't mean to imply anything . . . that is, I don't think *everyone* in Pakistan feels that way, but . . ."

"Racism can take many shapes, Kayla." He continued to smile as he opened his binder. "It's not simply about hating a group of people who don't look the same as you. It's about fear and misunderstanding, and judging someone without knowing all the facts. Once everyone realizes how foolish and destructive racism is, that is the moment it will come to an end."

CHAPTER TWO

LOOKING BACK ON A LEGACY OF HATRED

People of all races and ethnic backgrounds don't always have the same career opportunities.

The delegates at the convention center knew what they were up against when it came to fighting racism. They realized that discriminating against people because of their skin color or ethnic background dated as far back

*Many Jews died in Nazi concentration camps such as this
one, known as Auschwitz, during World War II.*

as ancient history. As Omar had stated, it was a problem rooted in fear,

hatred, and misunderstanding.

Victims of racism suffer everything from unequal educational and

career opportunities to acts of vandalism and violence. Because racism had existed for hundreds of thousands of years, Kayla, Omar, and the other attendees knew it couldn't be wiped out during the course of one meeting. How could they get people to feel or think differently in the long term about an issue that had plagued society for so long?

One delegate shared a particularly powerful, relevant personal experience. Juliana Goldberg was from the central European nation of Poland. She tearfully explained to the group why she had never met her great-grandparents. "I've seen photographs and have listened to the many wonderful stories my relatives tell of them," said Juliana, "but they died before I was born. They were murdered in 1941 because they were Jewish." During World War II (1939–1945), Germany's **Nazi** government was **anti-Semitic** and expressed its racial hatred by killing about 6 million European Jews in a tragedy that became known as the **Holocaust.**

"Unfortunately," continued Juliana, "I know that this problem isn't limited to bloodshed. Any time a person uses a hurtful name to describe someone of a certain skin color or even thinks he or she knows everything about him because of his ethnic background, racism is at work."

✢ ✢ ✢

Most historians agree that human beings have been affected by racial prejudice as far back as ancient Greece and Rome. But the majority of U.S. schools discuss early racism in the context of African slavery.

Beginning in the 1600s, many Africans were enslaved and forced to work on plantations in the United States and elsewhere.

Beginning in the 1600s and lasting until the conclusion of the Civil War (1861–1865), slavery involved millions of blacks being forced to labor on American plantations. When the war ended, men and women of color were technically free, but they continued to face many forms of prejudice, including **segregation**. They were subject to unfair laws and were generally excluded from the jobs, schools, and other public institutions that whites enjoyed. When blacks fought for a better place in society, their efforts were often met with violence and humiliation.

*More than 200,000 people participated in the civil
rights March on Washington in August 1963.*

During the 1950s and 1960s, however, many U.S. citizens participated
in what is now referred to as the **civil rights movement**. Under the
guidance of leaders such as Martin Luther King Jr., these individuals
marched and protested against racial discrimination. Their efforts helped
win improved treatment for African Americans.

Blacks are not the only group to have endured racism. World War
II involved the persecution of European Jews, as well as many Japanese

Americans. When Japan dropped a bomb on Pearl Harbor, Hawaii, in late 1941, the U.S. government responded by forcing more than 100,000 men and women of Japanese ancestry into special camps called war relocation centers. Officials claimed that the action was necessary to ensure that they posed no threat to the country. Though the majority of Japanese Americans were loyal to the United States, some people panicked. They assumed that anyone of Asian heritage was unpatriotic.

In the 21st century, racism is still evident in the United States and abroad. Following the terrorist attacks on the World Trade Center and the Pentagon on September 11, 2001, Middle Easterners and Muslims were frequently met with suspicion and hostility. Osama bin Laden, who organized the attacks, was a Muslim of Saudi Arabian descent. Some people jumped to the conclusion that all men and women who shared his background wanted to harm Americans.

Racists often express their hatred and ignorance through violence or the destruction of private property. They frequently use insulting names, called **slurs**, when referring to people of other ethnicities. Racists try to exclude people of different backgrounds from certain neighborhoods, schools, and jobs. They believe that they are better than, or superior to, these individuals.

In reality, racists are far from superior. In most cases, they are scared or feel threatened by cultures they don't fully understand or try to appreciate. They may have been raised with mistaken ideas or **stereotypes** about other races. Some may have had a negative experience with a person of a different ethnic background. That experience leads them to assume that everyone who shares that individual's background behaves the same way.

Whatever its causes may be, racism has a harmful effect on society. Today, groups exist to promote understanding, and many world leaders speak out against prejudice and discrimination. The fight against racism is ongoing. The real issue is determining the best ways to increase knowledge and acceptance so that this problem is cut off at its roots.

CHAPTER THREE

A Social Problem with Many Shapes

Members of the Ku Klux Klan stage a rally.

Adjusting her microphone, Kayla recalled Omar's thoughtful words: "Racism can take many shapes." She was preparing to talk about her grandparents' experiences with a white hate group known as the

Ku Klux Klan (KKK). Klansmen had planned to bomb the family store during the late 1950s after her grandparents participated in a civil rights march. On the evening the bombing was supposed to occur, a handful of local white business owners showed up to demonstrate their support for the Thompsons. The Klansmen must have been surprised by their presence because they didn't do more than shout a few slurs before disappearing into the night.

While she knew the powerful impact her story would have, Kayla was also learning that racism doesn't always reveal itself in bombs or name-calling. Juan Barros, a delegate from Puerto Rico, explained how his father had tried moving his architecture firm to a predominantly white area of Vancouver, Canada. But he ultimately had a hard time building a business there. Though no one was openly hostile, he suspected that some clients were reluctant to work with him because he was Latino.

There are different types of racism. All of them are equally destructive. Some groups, often called hate groups, openly and aggressively try to separate different ethnicities and races from the rest of society. Within the United States, the KKK terrorizes blacks, Jews, and immigrants. The men and women who belong to hate groups are obviously, or **overtly**, racist.

People who aren't racist base their frienships on shared
interests, not on the color of someone's skin.

Many other people who are prejudiced don't even realize or

acknowledge this aspect of their personality. They don't physically attack

anyone or destroy private property. They aren't comfortable using racial slurs in public. But they have unfair or incorrect attitudes about individuals of different skin colors or ethnic backgrounds. They do nothing to learn more about other cultures and simply accept as truths statements such as "All Middle Easterners hate Americans" or "All Americans are greedy and materialistic." These people don't necessarily equate their views with hatred and racism. Most of them would be surprised or offended to be labeled as racists.

Luckily, for every person who supports racism, there is a growing number of individuals dedicated to taking action to overcome it. These people don't pretend to know all the facts about each unique world culture, but they are willing to learn and are eager to find out. They accept differences in skin color or nationality, and celebrate them rather than fear or resent them.

Life & Career Skills

World citizens have come a long way in the fight to end racism, and their efforts are remembered and encouraged on March 21. In 1966, the UN declared that date the International Day for the Elimination of Racial Discrimination. UN leaders chose March 21 because six years earlier, South African police killed 69 peaceful demonstrators who were protesting apartheid, the country's official policy of racial segregation. Today, people use March 21 to host rallies, marches, speeches, and discussions designed to promote tolerance.

CHAPTER FOUR

THE IMPACTS OF INTOLERANCE

*Community members march together in an effort
to end violence in their neighborhoods.*

Kayla cleared her throat and began to tell the story of her grandparents'
near brush with racial violence. When she finished talking, the room
fell quiet.

"The most disturbing part," she continued, "is how that type of racism isn't completely dead. A friend of mine is Vietnamese. A racial slur was written on her mother's car after they moved to a new neighborhood. A few weeks later, someone destroyed their garden and broke the windows in their garage. Her family finally decided to move."

People who are overtly racist don't just hurt their targets when they express their hatred—they affect entire communities in the process. Hate groups who demonstrate intolerance by engaging in acts of vandalism, harassment, and violence are often guilty of committing crimes. Once this type of behavior occurs, a neighborhood's atmosphere becomes tense and unhappy.

Men and women who are overtly racist are so filled with anger and fear that they sometimes deal with mental health issues. Friends and loved ones regularly exposed to their message of hate are likely to be stressed and depressed. In especially sad

Learning & Innovation Skills

How does society track intolerance? The Southern Poverty Law (SPL) Center's Intelligence Project monitors hate groups and organized racist activity within the United States. Based out of Montgomery, Alabama, the SPL Center distributes information it collects to law enforcement officers, the media, and the general public. In 2006, it tracked 844 active hate groups within U.S. borders.

Tracking intolerance is just the beginning. What do you think communities can do to stop hate groups from spreading their negative views?

Racists convicted of vandalizing property or committing acts of physical violence are often sent to prison, but how does society fight back against racism in the workplace? In the United States and several other countries, people who believe they've been denied career opportunities on the basis of their race or ethnic background can file a lawsuit against an employer. Depending on the specific charges, companies found guilty of discrimination can sometimes be ordered to pay millions of dollars in compensation. If a person sues, however, he or she must prove that the employer's decisions were rooted in prejudice, and not related to actual job performance.

situations, members of younger generations who spend time with these racists begin mimicking, or copying, their behavior. They accept their belief system as sensible.

People may not always recognize or openly show their racism, but they can still have a negative impact on society. They make it difficult for individuals of other ethnic or racial backgrounds to enjoy the same social, career, and educational opportunities as everyone else. Though employers in most countries aren't supposed to discriminate against job applicants or employees because of their skin color, the practice still occurs. Even outside the workplace, all it takes is a disapproving look, a tasteless joke, or a presumption about a person's intelligence, abilities, or personality for racism to win out.

People who are victims of discrimination often resent the group that is judging them. As time passes, they start to develop their own prejudices and misconceptions. The results are

Kids learn their attitudes about people of other races from their parents.

frighteningly similar to those of overt racism. Entire communities—both local and global—lose the ability to embrace and appreciate each other's differences. Instead, they direct their attention to safeguarding their own feelings and way of life.

CHAPTER FIVE

MORE ACCEPTING WORLD CITIZENS

*School can be a good place to get to know people
from different racial and ethnic groups.*

"I think it would be great if everyone back home could hear some of the delegates to this meeting talk," she said. "Not just about racism, but about their countries and cultures."

"We already do something similar at my school," volunteered Juliana. "The student government brings in a guest speaker each month who has a different ethnic background. The speakers talk about their culture, and we get to ask any questions we want. We've hosted people from all over— Zimbabwe, Sweden, and the United States!"

"There are also several simple, everyday ways to combat racism," added Omar. "You would be amazed how easily you can get people thinking if you politely correct them when they make a racist or stereotypical comment. Half the time they're not even aware they're coming across as prejudiced, so you're actually doing them a favor by bringing it to their attention."

✢ ✢ ✢

Programs that honor diversity are just one way people are working to overcome racism and promote tolerance. Adults and young people work with groups ranging from student clubs to community organizations. They plan activities that explore and celebrate different races and ethnicities. Some libraries schedule reading events that focus on a new culture each week. Individual neighborhoods often arrange block parties to celebrate ethnic holidays such as the Chinese New Year or Mexican Independence Day.

Patiently explaining to someone why his or her opinion sounds intolerant may seem awkward at first, but it usually gets that person

to stop and think. People working to end racism in their day-to-day lives can set examples for other members of their community by forming relationships with individuals of all skin colors and ethnic backgrounds. Developing a friendship doesn't require much effort yet can go a long way toward demonstrating and promoting racial tolerance.

It's important to keep in mind that racism won't end quickly or easily, no matter how hard society fights to stamp it out. While it's easy to become frustrated and discouraged by ongoing acts of prejudice, it's important to never give up trying to create positive change. Many communities respond to vandalism, violence, and unequal treatment of different races by organizing peaceful marches, protests, vigils, and rallies. Citizens sometimes contact elected officials to express their desire for tougher antidiscriminatory legislation and harsher penalties for people convicted of racially motivated crimes. They offer support and comfort to victims of racism and attempt to help them realize that not everyone lacks tolerance.

✢ ✢ ✢

Kayla continued to think about the role she could play in ending racism as delegates to the summit prepared to wrap up for the day. "Omar, I wonder if you'd consider coming to Atlanta sometime," she said, as they walked out of the conference room together. "I'd love it if I could arrange for you to be a guest speaker at my school."

Colorful parades are part of Chinese New Year celebrations. Learning more about other cultures can help combat prejudice.

"Sure thing," replied Omar, smiling again. "My sister shouldn't be the only one in the family who gets to visit America!"

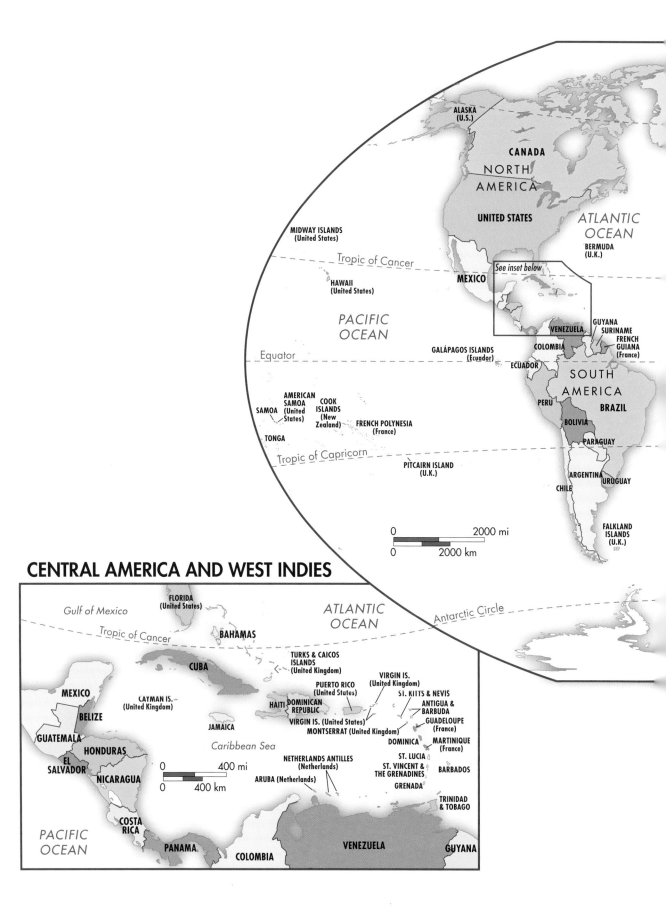

ALASKA
(U.S.)

CANADA

NORTH
AMERICA

UNITED STATES

ATLANTIC
OCEAN

MIDWAY ISLANDS
(United States)

BERMUDA
(U.K.)

Tropic of Cancer

MEXICO

See inset below

HAWAII
(United States)

PACIFIC
OCEAN

GUYANA
SURINAME
FRENCH
GUIANA
(France)

VENEZUELA

COLOMBIA

GALÁPAGOS ISLANDS
(Ecuador)

Equator

ECUADOR

SOUTH
AMERICA

PERU

BRAZIL

AMERICAN
SAMOA
(United
States)

COOK
ISLANDS
(New
Zealand)

SAMOA

FRENCH POLYNESIA
(France)

BOLIVIA

PARAGUAY

TONGA

Tropic of Capricorn

PITCAIRN ISLAND
(U.K.)

ARGENTINA

URUGUAY

CHILE

0   2000 mi

0   2000 km

FALKLAND
ISLANDS
(U.K.)

Antarctic Circle

CENTRAL AMERICA AND WEST INDIES

FLORIDA
(United States)

Gulf of Mexico

ATLANTIC
OCEAN

Tropic of Cancer

BAHAMAS

CUBA

TURKS & CAICOS
ISLANDS
(United Kingdom)

MEXICO

CAYMAN IS.
(United Kingdom)

PUERTO RICO
(United States)

VIRGIN IS.
(United Kingdom)

ST. KITTS & NEVIS

BELIZE

HAITI

DOMINICAN
REPUBLIC

ANTIGUA &
BARBUDA

GUATEMALA

JAMAICA

VIRGIN IS. (United States)

GUADELOUPE
(France)

HONDURAS

Caribbean Sea

MONTSERRAT (United Kingdom)

DOMINICA

EL
SALVADOR

MARTINIQUE
(France)

NICARAGUA

0   400 mi

NETHERLANDS ANTILLES
(Netherlands)

ST. LUCIA

0   400 km

ST. VINCENT &
THE GRENADINES

BARBADOS

ARUBA (Netherlands)

GRENADA

COSTA
RICA

TRINIDAD
& TOBAGO

PACIFIC
OCEAN

PANAMA

COLOMBIA

VENEZUELA

GUYANA

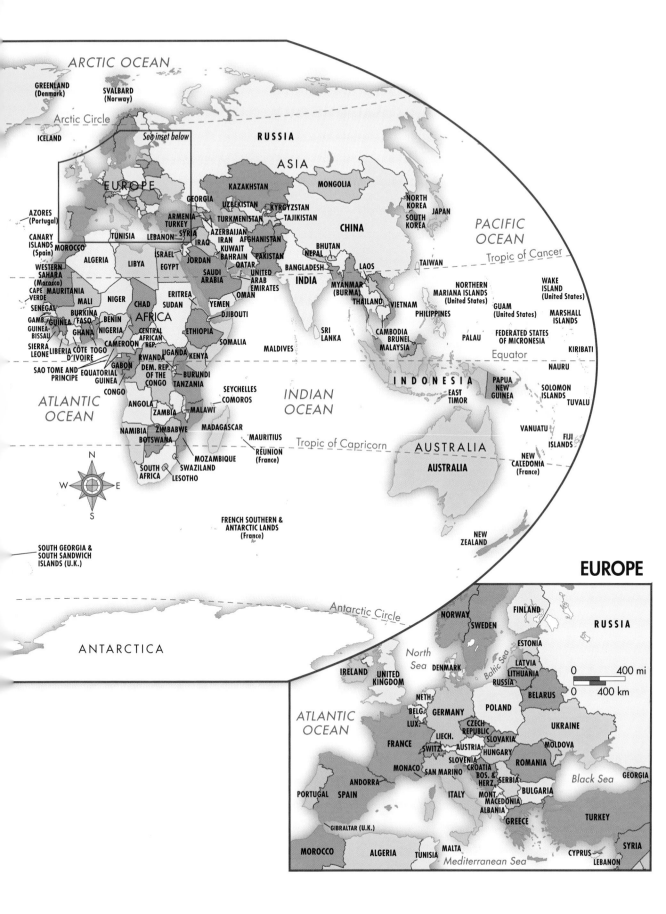

ARCTIC OCEAN

GREENLAND
(Denmark)

SVALBARD
(Norway)

Arctic Circle

ICELAND

RUSSIA

ASIA

EUROPE

AZORES
(Portugal)

KAZAKHSTAN

MONGOLIA

GEORGIA
ARMENIA
TURKEY
AZERBAIJAN
IRAN
AFGHANISTAN
SYRIA
IRAQ
KUWAIT
BAHRAIN
QATAR

UZBEKISTAN
KYRGYZSTAN
TAJIKISTAN
TURKMENISTAN

NORTH
KOREA
SOUTH
KOREA

JAPAN

PACIFIC
OCEAN

CANARY
ISLANDS
(Spain)

MOROCCO

TUNISIA

ALGERIA

LEBANON

CHINA

BHUTAN
NEPAL

Tropic of Cancer

TAIWAN

LIBYA

ISRAEL
JORDAN
EGYPT

PAKISTAN

BANGLADESH

LAOS

WAKE
ISLAND
(United States)

WESTERN
SAHARA
(Morocco)

SAUDI
ARABIA

UNITED
ARAB
EMIRATES

INDIA

MYANMAR
(BURMA)

VIETNAM

THAILAND

NORTHERN
MARIANA ISLANDS
(United States)

GUAM
(United States)

MARSHALL
ISLANDS

CAPE
VERDE

MAURITANIA

OMAN

PHILIPPINES

NIGER

MALI

CHAD

SENEGAL

GAMB.
GUINEA-
BISSAU
GUINEA

BURKINA
FASO

AFRICA

SUDAN

ERITREA

YEMEN

DJIBOUTI

SRI
LANKA

CAMBODIA
BRUNEI
MALAYSIA

PALAU

FEDERATED STATES
OF MICRONESIA

KIRIBATI

BENIN
NIGERIA

SIERRA
LEONE
LIBERIA

GHANA

CENTRAL
AFRICAN
REP.

CÔTE TOGO
D'IVOIRE

CAMEROON

ETHIOPIA

SOMALIA

MALDIVES

Equator

NAURU

SAO TOME AND
PRINCIPE
EQUATORIAL
GUINEA

GABON

RWANDA
UGANDA
KENYA

DEM. REP.
OF THE
CONGO

BURUNDI
TANZANIA

INDONESIA

EAST
TIMOR

PAPUA
NEW
GUINEA

SOLOMON
ISLANDS

TUVALU

CONGO

ATLANTIC
OCEAN

ANGOLA

ZAMBIA

SEYCHELLES

COMOROS

MALAWI

INDIAN
OCEAN

VANUATU

FIJI
ISLANDS

NAMIBIA

ZIMBABWE

BOTSWANA

MADAGASCAR

MAURITIUS

Tropic of Capricorn

NEW
CALEDONIA
(France)

AUSTRALIA

RÉUNION
(France)

AUSTRALIA

N

W   E

S

SOUTH
AFRICA

MOZAMBIQUE
SWAZILAND
LESOTHO

FRENCH SOUTHERN &
ANTARCTIC LANDS
(France)

NEW
ZEALAND

SOUTH GEORGIA &
SOUTH SANDWICH
ISLANDS (U.K.)

Antarctic Circle

ANTARCTICA

EUROPE

NORWAY

FINLAND

SWEDEN

RUSSIA

ESTONIA

IRELAND

UNITED
KINGDOM

North
Sea

DENMARK

Baltic Sea

LATVIA
LITHUANIA
RUSSIA

0   400 mi
0   400 km

BELARUS

NETH.
BELG.
LUX.

GERMANY

POLAND

LIECH.

CZECH
REPUBLIC

UKRAINE

ATLANTIC
OCEAN

FRANCE

SWITZ.

AUSTRIA

SLOVAKIA

HUNGARY

MOLDOVA

SLOVENIA

ROMANIA

MONACO

SAN MARINO

CROATIA
BOS. &
HERZ.
SERBIA

BULGARIA

Black Sea

GEORGIA

ANDORRA

PORTUGAL

SPAIN

ITALY

MONT.
MACEDONIA
ALBANIA

GREECE

TURKEY

GIBRALTAR (U.K.)

MOROCCO

ALGERIA

TUNISIA

MALTA

Mediterranean Sea

CYPRUS

SYRIA

LEBANON

GLOSSARY

anti-Semitic (AN-ti sem-EH-tik) driven by an intense hatred of Jewish people

civil rights movement (SIV-il RITES MOOV-muhnt) organized efforts during the 1950s and 1960s to end segregation and other forms of discrimination against African Americans

delegate (DEL-uh-get) a person chosen to represent others at a meeting

discriminated (diss-KRIM-uh-nate-id) treated unequally on the basis of a person's gender, religion, or race

Holocaust (HOL-uh-kost) extermination of 6 million European Jews and other civilians ordered by leaders in Nazi Germany during the 1930s and 1940s

intolerance (in-TOL-ur-uhntz) an unwillingness to accept and appreciate the customs and beliefs of different cultures, races, religions, and ethnicities

Islamic (i-SLAHM-ik) related to the religion of the Muslim people, whose faith is rooted in a holy book called the Koran and the teachings of the prophet Muhammad

Ku Klux Klan (KOO KLUKS KLAN) a white hate group targeting African Americans, Jews, and foreign immigrants

Nazi (NOT-see) a political party headed by Adolf Hitler and characterized by intense anti-Jewish principles

overtly (oh-VERT-lee) openly or obviously

prejudice (PREJ-uh-diss) the act of prejudging a person or group of people (often unfairly and based on factors such as race or ethnicity)

racism (RAY-siz-uhm) the act of discriminating against a person or group of people on the basis of skin color or ethnic background

segregation (seg-ruh-GAY-shuhn) when separate treatment or opportunities are given to people based on gender, religion, or race

slurs (SLURZ) hurtful or insulting names racists often use when referring to or harassing their victims

sociologists (soh-see-OL-uh-juhsts) scientists who study social institutions and development

stereotypes (STER-ee-oh-tipes) usually negative misconceptions that people apply to all members of an ethnic, religious, or cultural group different from their own

summit (SUHM-it) a meeting of leaders from different nations to address an international concern

FOR MORE INFORMATION

Books

Gifford, Clive. *Racism*. North Mankato, MN: Chrysalis Education, 2003.

Heinrichs, Ann. *The Ku Klux Klan: A Hooded Brotherhood*. Chanhassen, MN: The Child's World, 2003.

Sanders, Bruce. *Racism*. Mankato, MN: Stargazer Books, 2006.

Zullo, Allan, and Mara Bovsun. *Survivors: True Stories of Children in the Holocaust*. New York: Scholastic Inc., 2004.

Web Sites

Anti-Defamation League
www.adl.org
Read about how the Anti-Defamation League fights anti-Semitism, racial prejudice, and hatred all over the world

Global Issues: Racism
www.globalissues.org/HumanRights/Racism.asp
Learn about the different forms of racism throughout the world and what you can do to stop it

Tolerance.org
www.tolerance.org/about/index.html
Find out what you can do to fight hatred and bigotry, and promote tolerance

United Nations: World Conference against Racism, Racial Discrimination, Xenophobia and Related Intolerance
www.un.org/WCAR
Visit this Web site to find out about the steps that are being taken to end racism in the world

INDEX

ABOUT THE AUTHOR

Katie Marsico is a freelance writer and the author of more than 20 children's nonfiction books. She lives with her husband, Carl, and children, Maria and C. J., in a suburb of Chicago, Illinois. She dedicates this book to her dear friend Neyza Reyes.